For my sister Christa

In the light
of the moon
a little egg
lay on a leaf.

My Own
VERY HUNGRY CATERPILLAR
Colouring Book

by Eric Carle and _____

(write your name here)

PUFFIN BOOKS

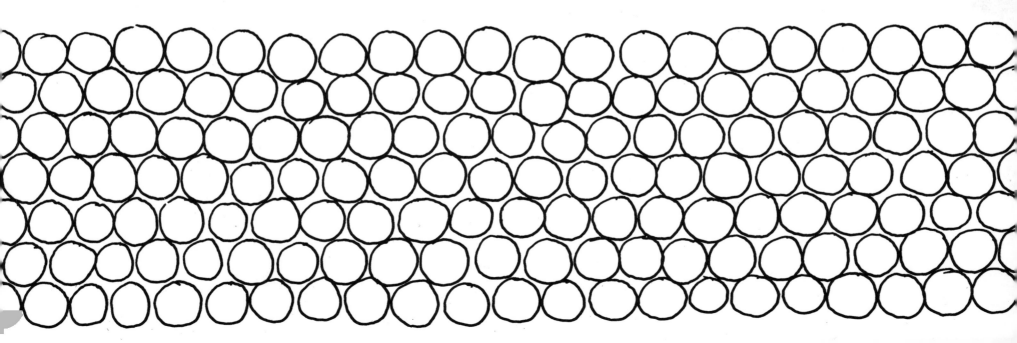

One Sunday morning the warm sun came up and – pop! – out of the egg came a tiny and very hungry caterpillar.

He started to look for some food.

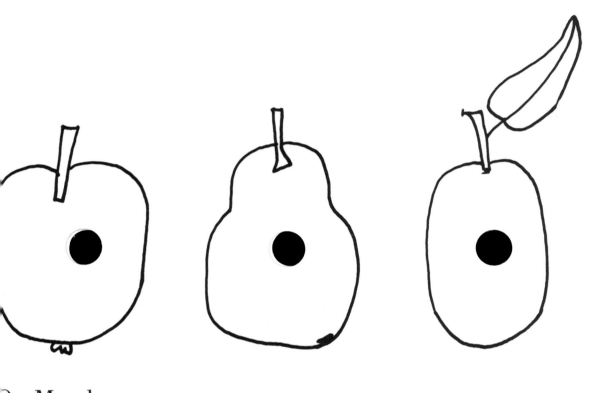

On Monday
he ate through
one apple.
But he was still
hungry.

On Thursday
he ate through
four strawberries,
but he was still
hungry.

On Friday
he ate through
five oranges,
but he was still
hungry.

On Saturday
he ate through
one piece of
chocolate cake, one ice-cream cone, one pickle, one slice of Swiss cheese, one slice of salami,

one lollipop, one piece of cherry pie, one sausage, one cupcake, and one slice of watermelon.

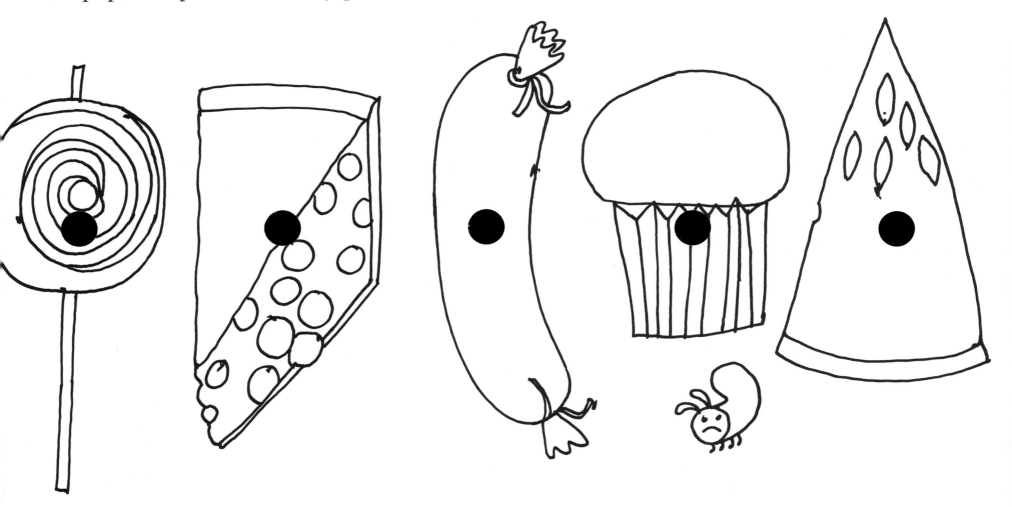

That night he had a stomachache!

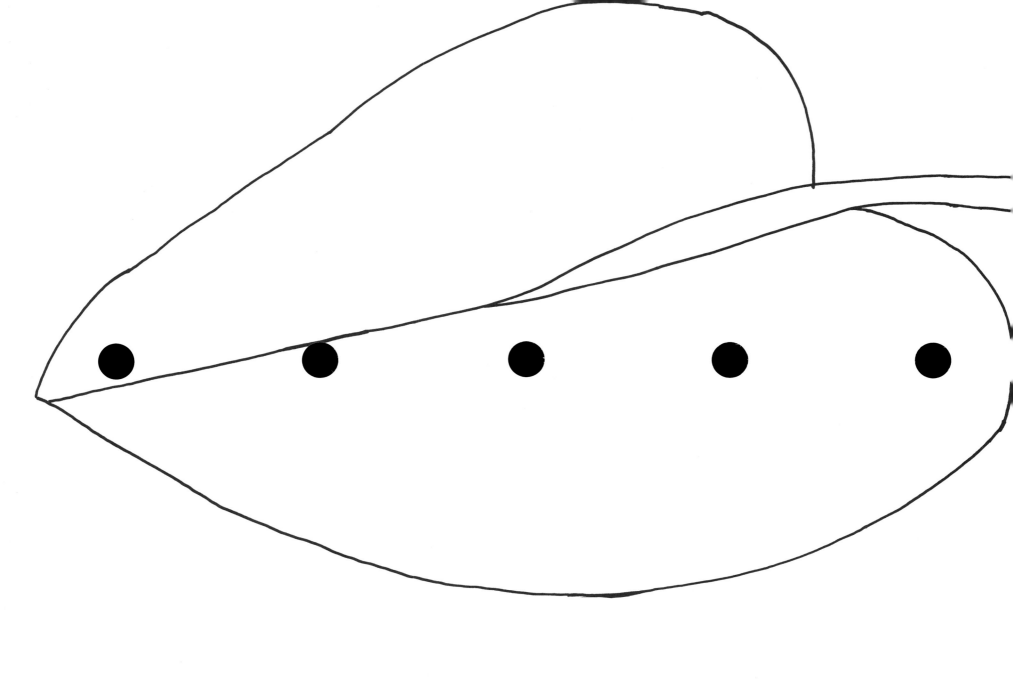

The next day was Sunday again.
The caterpillar ate through
one nice green leaf,
and after that he felt
much better.

Now he wasn't hungry any more – and he wasn't a little caterpillar any more.
He was a big, fat caterpillar.

He built a small house, called a cocoon, around himself. He stayed inside for more than two weeks. Then he nibbled a hole in the cocoon, pushed his way out and...

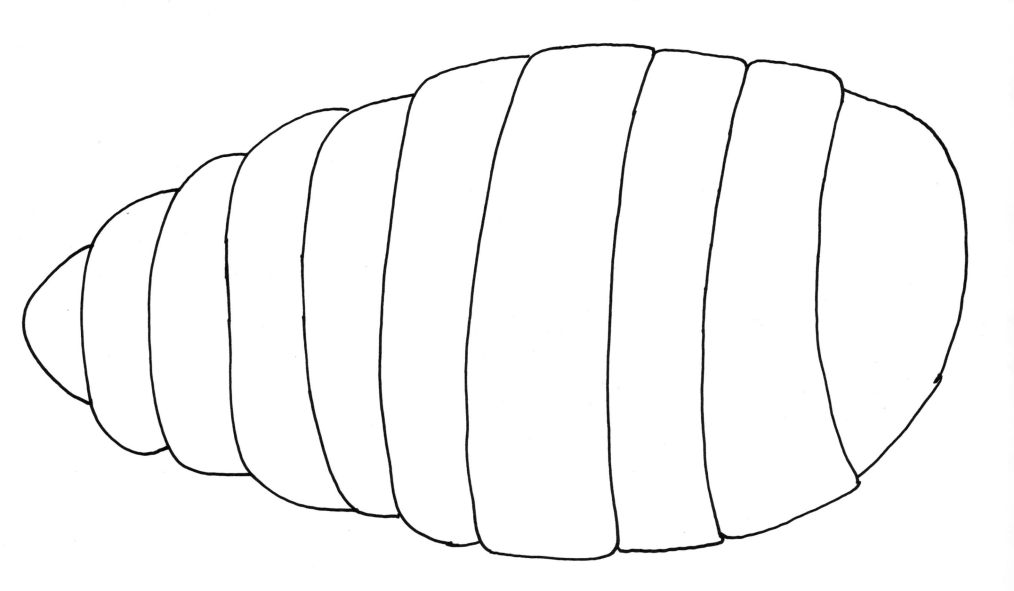

he was a beautiful butterfly!

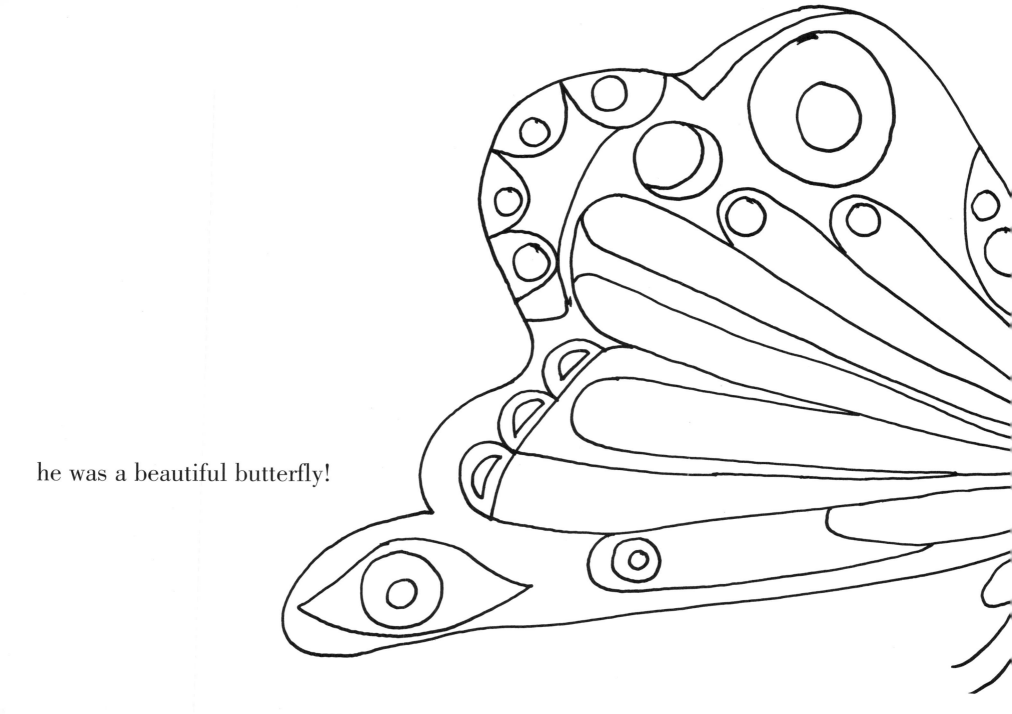

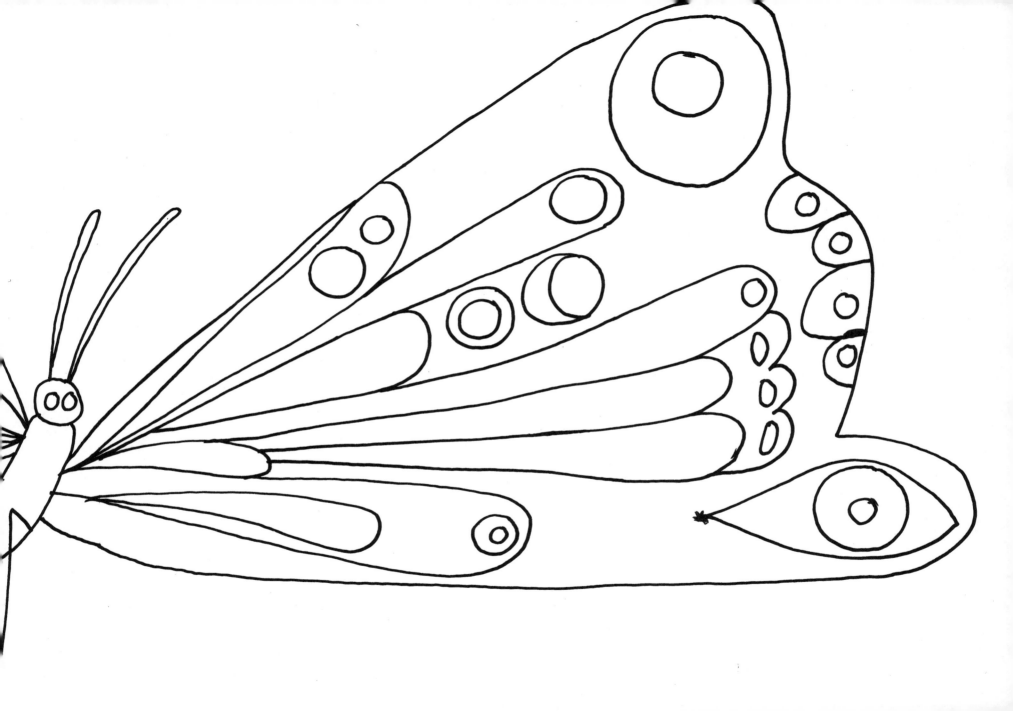

Eric Carle was born in Syracuse, New York, in 1929. His parents were German immigrants and in 1935 the family moved to Stuttgart, Germany. At the age of 16, he was admitted to an art school. This experience opened up a whole new world for Eric. Then, in 1952, he moved to New York City – which ended up being one of his favourite places to live. One day Eric showed an editor a story about a worm who eats holes through the page. The editor wasn't so sure about a worm. She thought another creature might be better. She said, "How about a caterpillar?" And Eric exclaimed, "Butterfly!" The rest, as they say, is history!

Place your photo here.

All About Me:

_____

_____

_____

_____

_____

_____

_____

I finished this book on _____ , _____ . I am _____ years old.

PUFFIN BOOKS

Published by the Penguin Group
Penguin Books Ltd, 80 Strand, London WC2R 0RL, England
Penguin Group (USA) Inc., 375 Hudson Street, New York, New York 10014, USA
Penguin Group (Canada), 90 Eglinton Avenue East, Suite 700, Toronto, Ontario, Canada M4P 2Y3 (a division of Pearson Penguin Canada Inc.)
Penguin Ireland, 25 St Stephen's Green, Dublin 2, Ireland (a division of Penguin Books Ltd)
Penguin Group (Australia), 250 Camberwell Road, Camberwell, Victoria 3124, Australia (a division of Pearson Australia Group Pty Ltd)
Penguin Books India Pvt Ltd, 11 Community Centre, Panchsheel Park, New Delhi – 110 017, India
Penguin Group (NZ), cnr Airborne and Rosedale Roads, Albany, Auckland 1310, New Zealand (a division of Pearson New Zealand Ltd)
Penguin Books (South Africa) (Pty) Ltd, 24 Sturdee Avenue, Rosebank, Johannesburg 2196, South Africa

Penguin Books Ltd, Registered Offices: 80 Strand, London WC2R 0RL, England

www.penguin.com

First published in the United States by Philomel Books, a division of Penguin Young Readers Group 2003
Based on *The Very Hungry Caterpillar*, published in 1969
Published in Great Britain in Puffin Books 2005
1 3 5 7 9 10 8 6 4 2

Set in Bodoni
Made and printed in the United States of America.

British Library Cataloguing in Publication Data
A CIP catalogue record for this book is available from the British Library

ISBN 0-141-50068-9

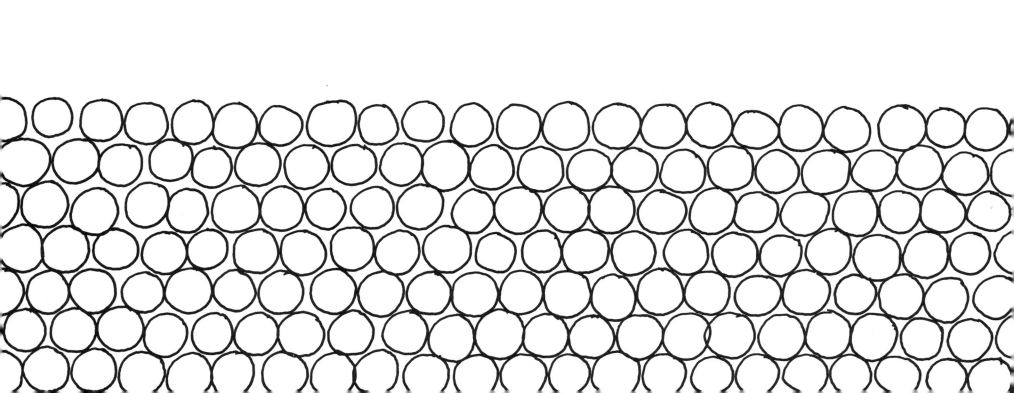

My very own drawings: